A SMALL HEAVEN

A SMALL HEAVEN

A MEDITATION MANUAL

JANE RANNEY RZEPKA

Boston
Skinner House Books

Excerpt from "Juggler" in *Ceremony and Other Poems*, copyright 1949, 1977 by Richard Wilbur, reprinted by permission of Harcourt, Brace, Jovanovich, Inc.

Library of Congress Cataloging-in-Publication Data
Rzepka, Jane Ranney
    A small heaven.

    1. Devotional—Unitarian Universalist churches. I. Title.
BV4811.R9 1988   242'.2 88-27938
ISBN 1-55896-122-4

Design by Suzanne Morgan
Editing by Mary Jane Curry

Contents

"It takes a skyblue juggler with five red balls
To shake our gravity up . . .
Swinging a small heaven about his ears."

—Richard Wilbur, "Juggler"

Introduction

In this collection, I offer you an ordinary year. The events described, and the observations, too, are ordinary, emerging from an ordinary universe of family and friends, past and present. I suppose my church, too, the Unitarian Universalist Church of Reading, would seem ordinary. But for me, these people, this world, are a wondrous small heaven, swinging about my ears. They are what shakes up my gravity, and for them, and for that, and for all who swing heavens in the lives of others, I am grateful.

—Jane Ranney Rzepka

Shaky Skaters

Roller World is a typical roller rink that rents foul-smelling skates with fragile laces, and then pounds your ears senseless with hard-driving rock music. Roller World caters to people with no standards, no taste, and no class.

Like my family and myself.

I love Roller World. No one was born to skate, but there we all are, a roomful of unlikely skaters, doing our best. A few of course are hot shots, whizzing around on one foot, backwards half the time, breezy as you please. And another bunch, sad to say, is hopeless—their eight little wheels completely ignoring mission control. But round and round the rest of us go, steady and solid, one foot and then the next, in careful time to the Beastie Boys or Twisted Sister.

Folks look pretty darn good out there. I suppose I do too. No one knows that if even one word is spoken in my direction, I will lose my concentration and hit the floor hard. No one realizes that if they come up behind me too fast I will panic and crumble into the wall. No one can see that this steady skater is so precarious that the act of skating, just skating, takes everything.

As we roll around the rink, uncertain of our stride and rhythm, may we yet see the instability of those who surround us. May we help when we are steady, holding those who falter; may we calm the reckless and urge the timid forward; may we keep gentle company with the skaters at our side. Let us move with the spirit of love, and may some quiet presence help us with our laces at the end.

Something I Could Count On

For as long as I can remember, as the days get longer, I get this funny feeling. I get the feeling the time's about to change. Moreover, I get the feeling that everyone else on the planet knows just when Daylight Saving Time begins. You all have the secret formula, you learned some clever nursery rhyme that tells when it happens, you all get a postcard in the mail from the office in charge of these Important Matters. But not me. Then the bad dreams start, the ones where I, blissfully in the dark, miss the spring time change and arrive at church Sunday morning just in time for coffee hour.

Last year I finally went to the library, investigated the Uniform Time Act, learned that the time always changes the last Sunday in April, wrote the date on a piece of paper, and put it in my top desk drawer, where I see it every single day. It feels good to be solidly in the know, settled.

But still I have the funny feeling that the time's about to change. Didn't I hear somewhere that they're changing the changing? Can they do that?!

I don't ask for much; I know nothing stays still these days: My uncle could marry a different aunt, my children could change their given names, my childhood home could one day become a parking lot, I could decide to become a donut maker or Roller Derby queen. I half expect all that. I'd just like a little something I could keep on a scrap of paper in my desk drawer, something I could count on.

Palm Sunday

This is what we get in life: We want and want and want—undying love, a world that is fair, eternal life for ourselves and those we care about—and we can't ever have them. We are faced always with a savior dead and gone and an empty tomb to prove it.

We have, I believe, been extended not salvation but mercy. Jesus' "reign of God" is with us—has been with us—radically, mercifully, all along in such forms as kindness, fairness, and wonder. We don't have to wait for Judgment Day, we don't have to be perfect, we don't have to be afraid; we need only look around and awaken to what has existed from the beginning of time.

We go on wanting and hoping and sometimes we are blessed. We don't get what we want—the tomb is still empty. Against that background every act of mercy is cause for rejoicing. One stalk of asparagus, a kiss, stirring music, a healthy morning, a good laugh, a kind touch—we have all that—and all of it, all of it, is holy.

Blessing the Blend

The sentence, "May we bring ourselves and our stories to church this morning, and consider the blend a blessing," appeared twice in our Palm Sunday service yesterday. I always believe what I say on Sunday morning, but I said this prayerful sentence in particular earnest, having lived through thirty-four or so Easter and Passover seasons in Unitarian Universalist churches.

Every year I fight the feeling that our UU churches just can't win on Easter. Our familiar congregation will come through the doors, alongside a number of Easter visitors we've never seen before. Why do they come?

> To hear familiar, traditional, Easter music.
> To not hear familiar, traditional, Easter music.
>
> To be reminded of the newness of spring, the pagan
>   symbols of the season, and the lengthening days,
>   without a lot of talk about Jesus and resurrection.
> To be reminded of Jesus and His resurrection, without
>   a lot of talk about the newness of spring, the pagan
>   symbols of the season, and the lengthening days.
>
> To participate in a family service, where children
>   delight in discovering the many roots of our
>   religious tradition.
> To participate in a dignified service, where adults
>   celebrate the undeniably Christian holiday,
>   Easter.

We each have religious stories, spring dreams, seasonal celebrations. And on Easter they're with us, joining together in church. It is our glorious celebration, and by considering the blend a blessing, we win every time.

Infinity Close at Hand

I was in an elevator—one of those glass elevators that zips along the outside of forty-eight floors. Looking down, one sees terraced floor after floor, blending into little horizontal stripes, finally descending into an all-too-clear view of infinity.

Nobody enjoys this, I'm convinced. Maintaining a confident, humanoid demeanor, what with all this infinity so close at hand, is trying. But it's possible...until the elevator stops mid-floor and begins an ear-piercing bleat. Minds go blank, overcharged with the electricity born of trying not to scream.

It all turned out fine, of course; we did slide down to some appropriate notch; the bleating stopped. I've ridden up and down the forty-eight floors a dozen times since, and the elevator ride is simply an elevator ride. But sometimes, for a split second, as in the rest of life, I look down past my shoes and see the infinity below. And I love my children and the green grass and everything else with all the intensity there is. Then the door opens in an ordinary way, and I get out.

Fragment by Fragment

My kids, and all kids, ask questions. It's a good thing. While I'm busy trying to cope with twentieth-century culture, they're still able to examine it. Today's questions:

> "Mom—the radio commercial just said, 'Don't you just hate it when you're walking down the street and you see someone wearing some really old-looking curls?' Can somebody's curls really ruin that lady's day?"

> "Mom—the TV section says '9:00, Channel 5, World Series if necessary.' How can you tell when the World Series is necessary and when it's not?"

> "Mom—the paper from school about music lessons says, 'Never make fun of the strange sounds that your child may produce.' Would parents really make fun of their children? Would you?"

Any ordinary question of this sort is likely to prompt a spontaneous sermon, so my children inevitably ask such questions poised with one foot out the front door, ready to run. There's religion in the everyday questions, and the kids know how much I value their gentle forays. Anaïs Nin wrote, "There are very few human beings who receive the truth, complete and staggering, by instant illumination. Most of them acquire it fragment by fragment, on a small scale, by successive developments, cellularly, like a laborious mosaic."

By asking about tired curls, the World Series, and strange sounds, the children find out what matters, what deserves attention, and how we might treat one another. They work on their mosaic, and they nudge me to keep working on mine.

With Eyes Wide Open

If you've ever had a CAT scan, that computerized series of fancy X-rays, you know what it's like. You're alone in a totally white high-tech room in a hospital, lying on your back, arms above your head, instructed to stay stock-still for forty-five minutes or so. The table you're on slowly moves into or through a machine that is round and white and smooth and sleek. The scanner surrounds you. There is no one to talk to. The room is still. There is nothing in your fixed line of vision except the uninterrupted surface of the CAT scanner. You see nothing at all, really, until your eye catches four or five holes, apertures of varying sizes, a few inches from your face. And around these holes, around the only points your immobilized gaze might focus its attention, is written, "Danger, laser activity, do not look at these holes!"

I'm always really sorry that I noticed those holes in the first place. It would have been so much easier not to have seen them, to believe the scanner was an unblemished surface unworthy of particular focus. Now that I know the apertures are there, I have to close my eyes.

In life outside the scanner, on the other hand, we can live with eyes wide open. An aperture comes into view—a concentrated window onto the cosmos at large, the mysteries of human nature, one person's soul, the perplexities of existence—and we can focus our eyes on the power. To be able to open our eyes to the immensity is one of our great blessings.

To Life Ordained

It was exactly ten years ago to the day that I first left my new baby, Adam, in someone else's hands for the evening. The memory is strong—the concern, the aching, the missing, pure and simple. There was not a part of me that wanted to leave that baby. But I did. I was being ordained.

It is the tenth anniversary of my ordination, and I want to write about what a special day it was. Ministers always do. They quote wise words that have held them in such good stead and recall the personal and religious gravity they felt during the service. I want to do that too. But all I remember is missing my baby.

I love the ministry and I loved being ordained into it. But my ordination was different: I learned that night about the power of caring, the wrench of separation, the ambiguity of responsibility, and the joy of reunion. Now and then a wise word or two comes back to me from that ceremony a decade ago, and the gravity, too. But mostly I remember how mortal I felt.

When Feet Flail

I read copies of old church minutes in our kitchen. If I put my mind to it, I can stand there and get through an entire annual report while waiting for whatever it is to boil. My observation thus far is this: We look on the sunny side.

In the entire history of our church, according to these reports, we have never had a murky dilemma, been a little short of cash, or even stumbled upon an intriguing situation. Except twice:

In 1935 the report mentions our organ music, which was lovely, despite the fact that the organist had lost "more than one finger" during his day-to-day activities as a local electrician. Whoa. I have a finger that doesn't work too well, and I'm filled with admiration for an organist who can play a few fingers short. But I'm not easily fooled—somebody must have been concerned for the man, if not for the music.

No problems appear as such, though, until 1980, when the "Pew Stabilization Committee" appeared. Seems the pews kept tipping over backwards. I had, frankly, always wondered why the congregation seems so alert Sunday after Sunday—I was on the verge of thinking it had something to do with the minister's preaching capacities. But it's all clear now—they were sitting in a pew, got kind of comfy—sleepy, too—their heads tilted back, mouths opened, they drifted off and *whoops*, the whole pewful went over, feet flailing in the breeze.

Wouldn't it be nice to imagine that missed notes and pew stabilization have been our greatest challenges? I feel sure, though, that we've endured tougher times, mercifully left unrecorded. One has to conclude that when the sun stopped shining, the organ stirred our singing nonetheless, and most feet stayed firmly on the ground.

My Boys at the Drugstore

So I said to my boys (aged eight and ten), "Well, . . . we can stop at the drugstore and buy some condoms so you can see what they are." I told them that I had never actually bought condoms before, and that I might feel embarrassed, especially if a lot of neighbors were standing around, and that people feel that way sometimes. We made a deal that if they felt embarrassed in the store, they could pretend never to have seen me before in their lives.

In the drugstore, one of my children said loudly, "Where would condoms *be*, Mom?" while the other headed straight for the pet food section and stayed there. There isn't much more to the story—we bought the condoms, took them home, Chuck and I talked a bit more with the kids, and nobody seemed to think a thing of it.

I used to say that I'm most comfortable being open with my children about sex. "That's my way," I'd say. "You do what's most comfortable for you." But now, the world has changed. Now I will say to you that your children need to know details about sex whether you're comfortable with that or not. Sex for them will need to be "safe sex." That must always be a given. Whether we like it or not, our children need to know about safer sex so they won't die.

The Mouse

This Sunday morning, as the prelude began, I was informed that a live baby mouse was in the wastebasket. In fact I was introduced, and this was one cute little mouse.

Remembering that ministers have graduate educations in a wide variety of areas, several members of the congregation were confident that I would know what the mouse should do next. And I did: It being 10:30, the little fella would get to stay right where he was and hear the sermon.

He did that, but by 11:30 those same members of the congregation were curious about what was next on the mouse itinerary. And again, I knew what to do: In my generosity, I would offer our student minister the opportunity to deal face to face with nature's wonders. She had it solved in five minutes flat. A couple of children would take it home. Kids happy, church happy, minister happy.

They were my kids. We were not keeping the mouse. No way.

At this writing, Sunday at 2:00, we have not spent a penny more than $30 on a "mouse habitat," food, and wood shavings. The pet store guy, mumbling something about bubonic plagues and such, sold us a "disease free" mouse. Chuck and I, in line for the "firm parenting award" ("Parents of Steel," Chuck calls us), are still looking for the original mouse, who escaped while we were at the pet store.

See? There's no problem I can't solve.

A special god exists, I think, who looks out for children who bring home pets—the same god who's in charge of triumphant love, inevitable springs, mechanical objects that work right, and all happy events. That god was on duty today.

Humanizing Mom

On Mother's Day, one expects to read about the wonder and glory of motherhood. While I can tell you from personal experience that we mothers like to be appreciated, I can also tell you that a rosy and sentimental Mother's Day column always refers to mothers in some other family—the picture painted there is not me, not my mom, not my grandmothers.

In my family, mothers do not suffer any more than other mortals, nor are we particularly unsung. We complain when we trip over shoes on the living room floor, and we expect a little praise for carrying the daily Grand Accumulation at the bottom of the stairs up the aforementioned stairs.

We do not deserve or expect devotion from our children. We wanted to have children. It was our idea. If they come around from time to time when they are grown-ups, we are ever so glad. But if they live their lives as secure and independent souls, we value that.

Motherhood, in my family, is not always the most important job in the world. Some of us are actually good at it, some of us shuffle along and do our best, and a few are better off in other professions. We try to face that.

Mother's Day is no time to romanticize parenthood—parenting is a down-to-earth process if ever there was one. So this Mother's Day, let's humanize Mom. Thank her for doing what she could, given all the dirty socks, thank her for loving you as well as she was able in spite of your three years in junior high, and then, let her thank you for the privilege of being your mother.

On Being Scared

I spent some time this weekend with an old friend, a dentist. She's considering buying her own practice, but wonders if she could retain the current patients and attract new ones. She wonders if the office staff would like her, or befriend her too much, or resent her, or desert her; she wonders about bill collecting, spending too much time on crowns and root canals (which she likes) at the expense of oral surgery (which she doesn't); she wonders about being a good wife and mother and all-around person. She's scared.

My friend is intelligent, well organized, energetic, terrific with teeth . . . but scared. It makes me think we all are. Scared we'll lose the company's big Formica account, scared we'll miss the time change, scared we're handling the kids' curfew wrong, scared our money will be in all the dumbest places when tax laws change, scared of our failing health, scared of everything falling apart, scared that nobody really loves us, scared of the fragility of all creation. Scared.

O Spirit of Life and Love, we aren't the giants we'd like so much to be, and the world can loom so large. When all is quiet and we are small and the night is dark, may we hear the tender breathing of all who lie awake with us in fear, that together we may gather strength to live with love, and kindness, and confidence.

The Girl Scout Cookie Truck

I couldn't believe it. It was warm out. Everybody around here pumped up their bike tires. Tiny crocus sprouts came up. Bats, balls, and baby carriages appeared. People raked. And yes, shucks, a couple neighborhood kids (including you know whose) got a little bit frisky and took apart old Mrs. Anderson's picket fence out back. I sat on our front steps, remembering days gone by in Berkeley and Ann Arbor when we all hooted at notions of marriage and "single-family dwellings," trying to decide whether it was a Norman Rockwell painting I was in, or a Martin and Judy Sunday School story.

Then, I swear, a trailer truck filled with boxes of Girl Scout cookies showed up. Too good to be true, for the purposes of my little vignette—heavy handed, I know—but there it was, and here came all the moms and dads and everybody to collect their stashes. I was warming up to the notion that, due to one of those time quirks popular in the movies, I was actually my mother and the year was 1955. Then reality reared its ugly head.

A guy in a van is livid that the Girl Scout cookie truck is blocking the street. The notorious neighborhood "pill" is livid that the guy in a van would dare use our street to avoid Main Street's traffic lights. Moms and dads are livid that the van guy and the "pill" are livid. Everybody jumps around and yells.

Spring is great: the sun, the balls and bats, the sprouting, those cookies. It's a wonder and a miracle, just like ministers say it is. But it's not salvation.

Stupid, Stupid Me

A woman in Rochester, New York, I read somewhere, mistakenly sold a cookie tin containing thousands of dollars' worth of jewelry at a garage sale. "I'm losing my mind," she said. "Stupid, stupid me."

The quotation, "stupid, stupid me," caught my eye for two reasons. First, I'm forever on the lookout for useful quotations. This one has already proved to be strikingly apropos on three occasions, and I've only had it an hour.

I circled the Rochester woman's observation for a second reason, this one worrisome: I have always made much of the Unitarian Universalist party line regarding "the inherent worth and dignity of every person." The notion of "valuing one another" creeps into the service in one way or another just about every Sunday morning. But sometimes, quite often in fact, we don't feel the least bit inherently worthy. At times we're far from dignified. To put it plainly, frequently we feel we're plain stupid.

The popular press is full of articles on low self-esteem. One would think even a half-alert minister would regularly acknowledge the condition and point out that people care about us even when we're turkeys. Who knows how it escaped my notice, dwelling as I do on my own stretches of ineptitude. Oh well, stupid, stupid me.

New Love in May

Somewhere I got the idea that Valentine's Day is part of our liturgical year, so every February I feel obliged to write about love. But who wants to write about love in February, when amorous inclinations are smacked by cold wind or mired in slush?

May's the time for love—just look around: Full grown adults wander around Quincy Marketplace, balloons in hand, in love. Perfectly normal people revert to goofy superlative statements about eyes, ear lobes, and the meaning of for-ever. The worst poetry and the gushiest songs ever written become woefully accurate. Nine-year-old boys gag. There is nothing more ridiculous, more real, or more blessed than new love in May.

In *Getting Married*, George Bernard Shaw wrote, "When two people are under the influence of the most violent, most insane, most delusive, and most transient of passions, they are required to swear that they will remain in that excited, abnormal, and exhausting condition continuously until death do them part." Okay—so we don't feel May's love in all our seasons; we're not designed that way. But to experi-ence the awe of early love even once, to feel its echoes over a lifetime, to glimpse that much of the divine, is a wonder worth writing about in May.

The Glove in the Subway

A one-paragraph newspaper article describes a subway platform during the morning rush hour at Grand Central Terminal. A train pulls in; a well-dressed woman gets off. Before the doors close, the woman realizes that she is holding only one of her leather gloves. She looks back into the train and spots the matching one on the seat. It is obviously too late to dash back in to retrieve it, so with a cavalier shrug, she flings her arm out and, the doors about to close, tosses her glove onto the seat alongside its mate. The doors shut, and the train pulls away.

What a great image. One could use it, I suppose, as a metaphor for facing the inevitable, or arguing for an orderly universe, or even, with a little stretch, for sharing the good things in life. But, as we move into the summer season, the metaphor that comes to mind is the one of "letting go."

To throw a favorite leather glove into the oblivion of a moving train must involve small pangs of uncertainty, pangs of some degree of loss, pangs of upset. After a lifetime of struggling not to lose our mittens, then our gloves, cavalier abandonment does not come easy.

In New England at least, our pattern is to cling, as we cling to our gloves, to routine, hard work, and obligation, all fall, all winter, and right through to the Fourth of July. But in the summertime, there is a letting go. We close up our schools and our churches, put our overcoats in moth balls, and dust off the swan boats, the lobster pots and last year's new gas grill. We need that. We need to cast that glove of responsibility back into the train. We need a vigorous and decisive toss about now to free ourselves of the confining gloves of life, even if we love them.

And the train's about to leave.

A Sport for Life

In a homework assignment designed to appeal to the sports-minded of the fourth graders, my son Toby's class was asked to make collages: "Use magazine pictures that show the sports activity you think you'd like best when you grow up." The collages poured in the next morning, snipped out dreams of pro football, baseball, and, from those children edging over four feet tall, basketball.

Toby chose pig-racing. Pig-racing!

I like that in a kid. Already, Toby knows that while popular sports are okay, he's apt to find a better dream for himself if he uses a little imagination.

I hope he remembers that lesson in life: to search out just the right dream, one that offers a pace and challenge that suits him, in spite of the choices others may make. Plenty of folks run around dribbling and punting and touching all the bases. But somebody's got to race those pigs. May it be my son.

The One That Got Away

I performed a wedding not long ago, and had a little trouble with the marriage license: it blew away. That's right—in all its signed, stamped, sealed and ready-to-go splendor, it, hoping no doubt to avoid eternal life in a file drawer, just sailed into the heavens on that windy wedding day and was never seen again.

So I went to Boston City Hall. Having had previous trouble proving conclusively that I was a "man of the cloth," I had my ordination certificate along. Having occasionally been suspected of I never knew quite what, I thought to bring the actual wedding ceremony, the couple's check, our parish register, church letterhead, and my driver's license. (I had a few nice wedding pictures along too, just in case.) But the woman said, "No dice. I have to see the 'church records.'" It did no good to point out that this hefty stack of offerings was the church records—she wasn't budging. Neither of us, it turned out, could imagine exactly what kind of "church records" would suffice. In fact, none would. She concluded that this was a problem that couldn't be solved.

I hated to go to jail, which is what I always figured happened to ministers who didn't properly file marriage licenses, so I kept at it. After a couple of hours, I, too, began to doubt that I'd ever performed the wedding, become a minister, or been born and given a name, though eventually the evidence did suffice.

As an adolescent, when I sometimes doubted my existence or my place in the universe, I turned to the existentialists if only to confirm the legitimacy of the doubt. But the actual healing came from the love, or even the nonchalant acceptance, of folks around me. May we remember to do that for each other.

23

The Still, Small Voice

And behold, the Lord passed by, and a great and strong wind rent the mountains, and broke in pieces the rocks before the Lord, but the Lord was not in the wind; and after the wind an earthquake, but the Lord was not in the earthquake; and after the earthquake a fire, but the Lord was not in the fire; and after the fire a still, small voice."
(1 Kings 19:11-12)

When you leave Filene's Department Store, a sign near the door reassures you, "For your convenience, an alarm will sound if the security device has not been removed from the merchandise." What?! If I were to stash, say, a dual-flow convector heater or a pastel sweatsuit under my coat and make off with it, Filene's would help me out, in a public spectacle, by blasting the kind of alarm that makes the eyes wild, the brain numb, and the hair flare in a thousand directions?

I guess so. Filene's figures the still, small voices are gone. "For your convenience," then, the store's security department offers to blow like the Lord's wind and shake like the Lord's earthquake to get the attention of our consciences. Presumably this blowing and shaking works well enough to protect the store, but alarms are no substitute for the voice that arises from within. The voice of the holy is ever in the still, small voice.

Along for the Ride

We Unitarian Universalists like to guide ourselves through life and its ultimate questions, to build our own theologies. We love the search, our individual quests. Every person in the pew decides about the divine, the nature of evil, and everything in between. It's a lot of work, but I've always bought the approach hook, line, and sinker.

Until last week, when we went white water rafting. They gave me a paddle—I could handle that. They gave me a wet suit—I got that on. They gave me a life jacket—I got that buckled up. They put a bright blue helmet on my head, showed me how to paddle, and put me in a raft in the Kennebec.

With a little practice and all of my attention and strength, I learned to follow the guide's commands. I stopped sliding around, paddled hard, and when I had the chance, bailed. The guide began to shout details about the water's configuration and possible approaches to each rapid. I was slow to understand that she expected us novices to take turns as guides!

I could cope with the cold, the wind, the rain. I didn't tire; I didn't conk anybody with my paddle. Simple shoeless camping in the woods along the bank was fine; worrying about the children was survivable; and I loved the rapids—even the scary ones. But that was my limit. On the river, I was along for the ride; I didn't want to guide.

At times in life, the water is choppy, the drops are sharp, and we're shivering hard and paddling fast. We can't always be our own guides. Sometimes it's enough just to sit there, along for the ride.

Enjoying My Shoes

I bought a pair of shoes the other day. The clerk put them in a box and then in a bag and said, "Enjoy them."

I haven't the faintest idea how to enjoy shoes. I have a long history of not feeling one way or another about my shoes. Certainly I've missed out on enjoying them.

Frankly, I feel a little naive. I always wondered why traffic was so bad on Friday afternoons—no doubt offices empty out early and people go home and enjoy their shoes. The malls are packed on weekends with what I now know to be people enjoying their shoes. Children scamper around the neighborhood, adults appear to be walking their dogs, runners pound the pavement, all, it now seems, for the pleasure of enjoying their shoes.

It's a good time of year for new and simple pleasures. Plant something new. Invent a fantastic ice cream concoction. Go to a ball game for a change. Set up the hammock and use it this time. Buy a different kind of book. Spend an extra ten minutes with a person you love. Feel the breeze. Wear some weird color. Turn the music up. And the lights down. Find something that smells terrific. Invite someone over without cleaning the house and discover that they still like you.

Go ahead and do all that. Me, I'm going to enjoy my shoes.

The Pillow

Last summer, when our family was visiting Maine, we slept wonderfully well. We just couldn't get over how soft the pillows were! I was so impressed, in fact, that I dug out a Vermont Country Store catalog and immediately ordered a couple of feather pillows—the softest they make.

One fine day the pillows arrived. After a lot of fanfare, I curled up for a nap, and yes, it was indeed the softest, most restful pillow on earth.

But it smelled funny.

The pillow drove me crazy. I couldn't place the smell—but finally, lying there half-awake one night, the smell took me to Wisconsin, to my sister's farm. I knew what the feather pillow smelled like. It smelled like a chicken coop!

Sometimes in life we get exactly what we ask for. I ordered a feather pillow and I got a pillow that smelled like feathers. We get what we thought we wanted; it doesn't seem right somehow; and the problem is so obvious that we can't even see it—or smell it. Whoever said that we make the bed and then have to lie in it, has a point.

Bursts of Splendor

On an airplane recently I sat next to a science teacher from San Francisco. Twenty-four years old, flying east for the first time, the young man was eager to experience autumn. He'd never seen leaves change color.

He went on and on about this: "In pictures, some of the leaves look red. I just can't believe they could turn bright red!" I, meanwhile, was trying to write a meditation for Sunday morning, along the lines of appreciating the glory and the beauty that is ours at this time of year—I wanted him to pipe down. But no, he continued with his incredulity, his delight, his boyish anticipation of the prospective spectacle.

I couldn't imagine the young science teacher happier than he already was, but as he spoke to me of his plan for his friends, he really began to glow. He had decided that he would choose one special brilliantly colored leaf for each friend, and make a little gift of it when he returned home. In six weeks.

Teacher of science though he was, he hadn't learned that bursts of splendor never last. He was too young, I guess, and too giddy.

And I couldn't tell him.

Spirit of transient joy,
Spirit of utter delight,
Our hearts are often anguished and bruised.
May we embrace your glorious moments as if they were
    forever,
And if we be too innocent, may we be gently forgiven.

Notes from the Zoo

I spent a day at the Brooklyn Zoo. It just happened that way. And when it happens that a minister spends the day at the zoo, I believe it is customary for that minister to observe that animals remind one so much of people (though not, of course, of members of the congregation).

Well, it's true. We and the other animals have a lot in common, a lot to discuss, and a lot to learn from each other. In the brand new jungle exhibits, I learned three things (which far exceeds my usual learning limit during days off with the family).

An elephant's gestation period is almost two years. Two years, according to the guide, is a pretty long time to be pregnant. (I had to agree.) But eventually, after what must take enormous patience and some very hard work on the big day, a beautiful infant weighing at least 125 pounds is born. The elephants reminded me that big, beautiful projects, of nearly any description, require a long wait.

I saw a rhinoceros up close. It's skin seemed thicker than any skin I'd seen on anything during my thirty-five years. The guide knew people take one look and think "thick skin," so he told us how sensitive rhino skin is to sun and insect bites. The rhinos reminded me that the thick-skinned feel pain like the rest of us.

The tapir looks like a gigantic pig and escapes extinction in several countries where, for religious reasons, people avoid eating pork. But tapirs are actually related not to pigs, but horses. The tapir reminded me that the right thing often happens for the wrong reason.

A foliage tour on Columbus Day? Maybe, but I recommend the zoo.

Let the Woman Decide

I worked in family planning clinics for six years in California. In these times, when violence erupts in response to
the availability of abortion, I want to speak about it.

My first job was counseling. After a woman's positive preg-
nancy test, we'd talk about the options. Maybe she was
thrilled. Or maybe she was horrified and knew she would
choose to abort. Or she may have needed to wrestle with
her beliefs, emotions, and circumstances before deciding.
In any case, it was my job to help her sort things out.

Later I rotated through the other jobs: assisting in the oper-
ating room, coaching, and cleaning up. Other times I was
clinic supervisor, worrying about the narcotics, the lab
reports, how to deal with an irate family member, how to tell
a sixteen-year-old she is too far along for an abortion.

I became very opinionated. I developed strong feelings
about every aspect of abortion from instrumentation to post-
operative care. But not once—never—did I form an opinion
about what a particular woman should do. Did she make
the right decision? I never knew the answer.

I never knew the answer! I couldn't know or see or predict
all, so I *couldn't* know the answer. A woman's decision is
sacred turf. No advice can be given. We each formulate an
opinion from our own little corner of the world, and act on it
with integrity. The best we can do is to protect the right
each of us has to choose our own course, to make our own
decisions about parenthood.

Knowing our own limitations, accepting the humility that
comes with being human, understanding that we do our
best in a less than perfect world, may we love and accept
each other above all else.

Revenge

One October day, just before dinner, in a bit of a rush, my son Toby, then aged five, and I went up to the attic to find Halloween costumes. My husband shouted up that he and Adam would make a run to the grocery store and do a quick cart's-worth of shopping. Toby and I unpacked the clown, witch, and superhero suits, anxious to establish our new identities before it got any colder or darker, there being no heat or lights in our attic. Chuck ran to get his wallet, momentarily folding up the attic stairs as he went by.

Well, it should have been momentarily. It was perfectly quiet downstairs. Soon, it was perfectly dark in the attic. There was no way to get the ladder unfolded from above. The phone rang. The paperboy came to collect. The dog needed to go out. The water for the broccoli had boiled away. I had a whole hour to think of an appropriate reaction to my husband when he walked in the door.

Revenge crossed my mind. I could somehow lure him into the attic and close it up and see how he liked it. Good old-fashioned ancient-Greek-type blood revenge. Or perhaps a little ancient Hebrew eye-for-an-eye proportional retribution, along the lines of domestic sabotage—a raw egg in the picnic lunch, salt in the sugar bowl, that kind of thing. Then there was forgiveness, Jesus' option. I could just say, "No problem, Chuck, I've never had the opportunity to spend some quiet, dark moments with Toby in our attic before."

Sometimes it's best just to forget. No energy spent on vengeance, no energy spent on forgiving either—a laugh maybe later, nothing more, and it all slips away.

Pilgrim Winslow

Apparently Pilgrim Edward Winslow wrote the only eye-witness description of the first Thanksgiving. In his brief letter to a friend in England, Winslow described the joy, the celebration, and the carousing that followed the harvest of 1621. That first to-do seems to have been like "Harvest Home" back in England: "cakes and ale and hang the cost."

Pilgrim Winslow makes no mention of thanks!

Uh-oh. We find out that the religious component of Thanks-giving, and even the act of giving thanks, are later additions. Isn't that the way?

At any given time, we're busy with our cakes and ale and turkey feathers. It's only later, looking back, that we under-stand the gravity of our harsh winters, the fragility of daily life, the preciousness of hopes for years to come. We get through it, we celebrate, and then, finally, the thanksgiving comes.

Important Notice

The newsletter editor of the First Parish in Wayland, Massachusetts, recently ran her favorite *New Yorker* squib:

"IMPORTANT NOTICE. If you are one of the hundreds of parachuting enthusiasts who bought our *Easy Sky Diving* book, please make the following correction: On page 8, line 7, the words 'state zip code' should have read 'pull rip cord.'—Adv. in the Warrenton, (Va.) Fauquier Democrat."

I worry about things like this during the Christmas season. Had I been a parachuting enthusiast, and had I breezed through *Easy Sky Diving* during the month of December, I'd still be flying through the air, picking up speed, shouting my zip code.

Zip codes aren't important. Rip cords are. During the Advent season, it's all too easy to confuse one for the other. The "zip codes" of the season—the replacement bulbs, the four sticks of butter, the fruit-by-mail catalogs, the party shoes—have our attention, and before we know it, we're picking up speed and shouting out those "zip codes" without ever asking why.

Perhaps we should look to our rip cords. Our lifelines, in December as always, are our inner quiet, the love we exchange, and our efforts to make the world more whole. We can slow the descent. We can take in the view. And we can anticipate a gentle landing on the twenty-fifth.

The Christmas Spirit

Newsletters from other churches arrive in the mail every day. So I read them, and they get me to thinking. For example:

Ministers' columns at this time of the year say one of two things: "The holiday season is a happy time," or "The holidays are depressing." The "happy time" school of thought makes a case for generosity, good cheer, and a deepening spirituality, whereas the "depression" advocates cite studies that prove the winter holidays are difficult. At the moment, the "happy holidays" group has a slight edge, the freshest crop of Ph.D.s having studied our December moods and found them to be merry after all.

I beg to differ. With no empirical work at all to back me up, I'd like to make a case for people being regular people even when December rolls around. Sure, Mom is frantic after Thanksgiving, but she is a frantic person in general. Brother John is nonchalant about the holidays, but he's always been the laid-back type. Aunt Martha gears up for a family squabble, but remember, she set up a round or two in July. Uncle John is a natural Santa, but he's a sweetie all year long.

In our family, we will incessantly exclaim, "Where's your Christmas spirit?" from Thanksgiving until the twenty-fifth. This phrase, at our house, has always been an obnoxious code for "Lighten up, it's Christmastime, act merry, not human."

I'm changing the code. This year "Christmas spirit" will refer to the fact that we are who we are, merry or depressed, and we love each other anyway.

Great Gifts Under $25

The perennial question is how to avoid being over-whelmed by the holiday season. Far be it from me to suggest that this is a "woman's question," but a glance at the newsstand reveals these feature articles in December's women's magazines: "300 Ideas for the Best and Happiest Christmas Ever" (*Family Circle*); "323 Great Gifts for Under $25" (*Good Housekeeping*); "112 Cookie Recipes" and "10 Ways to Look Dazzling for the Holidays" (*Ladies' Home Journal*); and "50 Ways to Cut Holiday Costs" (*Woman's Day*). Does this look like holiday spirit to you? To me it looks like work—if not guilt, anxiety, and confusion.

I don't mean to be a Scrooge; I love the winter holidays. My goals, however, are less ambitious than the magazines': I'd be happy with only one or two ideas for a "very good" Christmas; one real possibility for a gift under $25; one good cookie recipe that doesn't call for refrigerating the dough; and a few ways to look alert and alive ("dazzling" is out of the question) for the holidays.

The *Boston Globe*'s "Confidential Chat" column suggests we save this year's wrapping paper to glue on next year's Kleenex boxes. No one suggests paying some attention to the haunting vision that appeared to the Judean shepherds almost 2,000 years ago, or to the universal significance of the ancient December festivals of darkness and light. Few articles remind us of the simple beauty of a wreath or the memories that the old songs and stories unearth. Good will and giving are overlooked. These, to me, are the "ideas for the best and happiest holiday season ever." These are the "great gifts under $25."

Myth and Miracle

This is going to sound like an Easter message, a trifle defensive in tone, that responds to the imaginary critics who chastise us for finding meaning in the Easter story though we may not believe it happened. Or they tease us about our icky spring/bunny/daffodil talk, as though we're trying to celebrate Easter, but doing it wrong. About the time my spirit wants to soar with Alleluias and rebirth, with myth and natural miracle, those imaginary voices complain about Biblical literalism on the one hand or plain theological denial on the other.

Christmas works the same way. Myth and nature. We have a religious story of the birth of a holy baby, and we have the miracle of the lengthening days. Critics like to smirk at one or the other. But not me. I go for the myth and the miracle one hundred percent.

A baby was born, the story goes. The baby was special. The baby would bring peace and justice and love. Everyone around was amazed by the child, awed. The baby brought hope. The people knew joy. I love this story. I love it not because I believe a virgin bore a Newborn King on 12/25/0; I love it because it reminds me of the ancient wisdom of celebrating human greatness and holiness.

And the lengthening days. The lengthening days! How can anybody say "Bah humbug" to the very light itself? Together on Christmas we light our little candles so that the world might seem less bleak, we might feel less afraid, and flickers of safe expectation might again come our way.

I can't think why I'd want to hold back at Christmastime. So I wish you each a season full of infant-hope and steady light. Merry Christmas!

The Choice

One of the most obnoxious dilemmas a parent can present is "Well, you can have your choice. You can come in to the petting zoo (cousin's recital, ocean, store, camper, ballet) and have fun with us, or you can sit and sulk in the car."

You remember. There were parts of the petting zoo, recital, ocean, mall, camper, or ballet, that you didn't like. The frisky goat that knocked you over, the perky Mozart, the ocean slime that got in the way of your good time. Yes sir, alone in the car, nobody was going to make you get butted or bored or green. Pouting had an appealing integrity. Until the family returned. Turned out they really did have a good time.

The winter holidays give us religious liberals the chance to be that kid again, the kid with The Choice. In our church, we recognize Chanukah—though some out there no doubt find teeny colored candles annoying. In our church, we make mention of the solstice, though a few folks do prefer the dark. In our church, we celebrate Christmas, though a few among us despise the carols.

I hope you will join in the season of celebration. It won't be perfect. But a special tree somewhere, lights in the darkness, or a simple menorah; the miracle of new birth, the blessings of freedom, the promise of new light—something, something—will be a wonder. It's enough to get us out of the car.

They're Betting on a Storm Tonight

Tonight New England is bracing for a big storm. A "one-two punch," they're calling it; snow first, then bitter cold. For some reason, this comes as quite a surprise to us here in New England.

New Englanders, you see, have a little secret: We each think that we've chosen to live out our life at a sensible latitude. Granted, looking at a map, one gets the impression that we've placed our dream homes, loved ones, and expensive vehicles, square in the middle of large banks of snow. But cartographers have simply made a silly error in computation—we're not planning on festooning *our* lives with snow, not here in New England!

So, like last week and the week before, the radio is predicting a good bit of snow. In Buffalo, or Flint, or Cody, of course, snow in the winter isn't worthy of much mention. But here in Boston, we like to gear up for such an event.

We huddle and we cheer each other on, we fret and we frown, we protect what wants to live and draw our first loves close. In our own separate ways, we gather in all warmth and stand firm against the storms.

They're betting on a storm tonight.

Frogs and Firm Foundations

Won I remember growing up, I picture being outdoors. In Ohio for three days one week, our children, trudging through the deep crusty snow, got the tour. "This is where Mommy:

made pottery out of real mud/clay and baked it in the sun;
caught fifteen frogs in one day, and then wondered why;
felt the best, most trusted, swinging grapevine collapse
    over a ledge on an otherwise perfectly normal day;
followed a brook through the woods in search of the Erie
    Canal and—maybe—Japan;
discovered the strangest thing ever: echoes;
camped alone in the woods for as many days as she could
    without coming in, and once got hopelessly lost and
    lonely;
chewed on sassafras leaves and Allegheny birch twigs and
    thought everybody did—and don't they still taste
    good;
fell through the ice and was so damn cold;
found wild flowers that took her breath away, but kept it
    secret, feeling guilty always that she didn't let the
    Cleveland Plain Dealer know;
swam in the river in the pitch dark with girlfriends, each
    with hair in gigantic rollers;
and played tough Saturday basketball with friends in a barn
    and nothing was more important."

The kids just looked at me, the way kids do. But to me the earth seemed more solid that day, and the foundations never seemed firmer.

The Idiocy of Flight

A well-known poem by Robert Graves speaks of butter-flies—their "honest idiocy of flight," "lurching here and there by guess and God and hope and hopelessness." Any number of quotations sound this way, and so, I think do we. But privately.

Publicly we speak the civilized language of human beings who have things under control. No idiocy, no lurching. The world sees that we function well and happily. Other people believe it, and even we begin to believe it. Life moves forward as always.

Privately, though, we experience long stretches of turbu-lence and the occasional sudden downdraft. So many in our church feel alone when things go poorly at home, when they feel their age (whatever it is), or when they grieve. So many feel alone in their money worries or career problems. Awful life situations seem to set us apart from one another.

Normal lives include these awful parts. They don't always show from the outside; it's hard to believe any other folks at coffee hour are feeling the same kinds of screaming pain, or emptiness, or entrapment, or panic, or precariousness, or low-grade worry. Lives, even lives well-lived, don't stay in place for long—at least that's how it seems from the peculiar vantage point of the minister's study.

It's a help, I think, to accept "the idiocy of flight," the butter-fly flight-pattern so firmly implanted in the human mind and heart. Let the lurching, then, be no surprise, and know we're all up there flying every which way, together.

About Unitarian and
Universalist Meditation Manuals

For nearly 150 years, the Unitarians and Universalists have published annual editions of prayer collections and meditation manuals. After favoring theological topics in the early years of the denomination, in 1841 the Unitarians published *Short Prayers for the Morning and Evening of Every Day in the Week, with Occasional Prayers and Thanksgivings*. Over the years the Unitarians published many volumes of prayers, including several editions of Theodore Parker's selections. The current tradition of an annual lenten manual began in 1938 with *Gaining a Radiant Faith* by Henry H. Saunderson.

Several Universalist collections appeared in the early nineteenth century. A comprehensive *Book of Prayers* was printed in 1839, featuring both public and private devotions. During the late 1860s, the Universalist Publishing House was founded to publish denominational materials. Like the Unitarians, the Universalists published lenten manuals, and in the 1950s they complemented this series with advent manuals.

Since the merger of the Unitarians and the Universalists in 1961, the lenten manual has evolved into a meditation manual, reflecting the theological diversity of the two denominations. Today the Unitarian Universalist Association meditation manuals alternate between two styles of collections: poems or short prose pieces written by one author—usually a Unitarian Universalist minister—and anthologies of work by many authors, edited by one person.

The following list includes all meditation manuals since the merger, plus Unitarian titles prior to 1961. Unfortunately, there is no definitive list of earlier Universalist titles.

1970   *Beginning Now* J. Donald Johnston

1969   *Answers in the Wind* Charles W. McGehee

1968   *The Trying Out* Richard Kellaway

1967   *Moments of Springtime* Rudolf Nemser

1966   *Across the Abyss* Walter D. Kring

1965   *The Sound of Silence* Raymond Baughan

1964   *Impassioned Clay* Ralph Helverson

1963   *Seasons of the Soul* Robert T. Weston

1962   *The Uncarven Image* Phillip Hewett

1961   *Parts and Proportions* Arthur Graham

1960   *Imprints of the Divine* Raymond Hopkins

1959   *Indictments and Invitations* Robert B. Cope

1958   *Strange Beauty* Vincent Silliman

1957   *Greatly to Be* Francis Anderson, Jr.

1956   *My Heart Leaps Up* Frank O. Holmes

1955   *The Task is Peace* Harry Scholefield

1954   *Taking Down the Defenses* Arthur Foote

1953   *My Ample Creed* Palfrey Perkins

1952   *This Man Jesus* Harry C. Meserve

1951   *The Tangent of Eternity* John Wallace Laws

1950   *Deep Sources and Great Becoming* Edwin C. Palmer

1949   *To Take Life Strivingly* Robert Killan

1948   *Come Up Higher* Hurley Begun

1947   *Untitled* Richard Steiner

1946   *The Pattern on the Mountain* (Reissue)
         E. Burdette Backus

1945   *The Expendable Life* Charles G. Girelius

1944   *The Disciplines of Freedom* Leslie T. Pennington

1943   *Faith Forbids Fear* Frederick May Eliot

1942   *Forward Into the Light* Frederick W. Griffin

1941   *Victorious Living* W. W. W. Argow

1940   *Address to the Living* Herbert Hitchen

1939   *The Pattern on the Mountain* E. Burdette Backus

1938   *Gaining a Radiant Faith* Henry H. Saunderson

These and other publications are available from the Unitarian Universalist Association. For a free catalog, write to the UUA Bookstore, 25 Beacon St., Boston, Massachusetts 02108-2800.

Dawn to Dusk
Jacob Trapp
Gentle, thoughtful meditations by the minister emeritus of the Unitarian Church of Summit, New Jersey. (Trapp) 1984. 78 pp. Pb.

Exaltation
Edited by David B. Parke
The 1987 UUA meditation manual collects poems and prayers of UU ministers and lay people. Many selections appeared originally in *Voices Shaken from the Yew Tree: A Book of Lenten Meditations*, privately printed by the First Unitarian Church of St. Louis in 1986. 40 pp. Illustrated. Pb.

Finding Foxes
Terry Sweetser
Popular sermon collection by the former minister of the UU Congregation of Atlanta. Sweetser invites us to join him in his search for meaning in life, and urges us to become the people we wish to be. (Rising Press) 1985. 151 pp. Pb.

Forward Through the Ages
Dana McLean Greeley
Probing, insightful, sometimes funny sermons from 1970 to 1986 by the former UUA president. Edited by his parishioners at the First Parish in Concord, Massachusetts. 1986. 179 pp. Pb.

Generation to Generation
Tom Owen-Towle
A father passes along wisdom and humor to his children in this "ethical will." (Sunflower Ink) 1988. 143 pp. Pb.

Giving Life to Meaning
Terry Sweetser
Third sermon collection by this popular minister. Sweetser
explores the UUA Purposes and Principles covenant and
notices "how commonplace experiences can meaningfully
connect us to the interdependent web of existence."
(Rising Press) 1987. 144 pp. Pb.

The Numbering of Our Days
Anthony Friess Perrino
Thirty-nine meditations span the year from Ash Wednesday
to Valentine's Day. Sometimes funny, occasionally sad,
these poems, prayers, and provocations provide a rich and
thoughtful assortment of readings for many occasions.
1987 UUA meditation manual. 64 pp. Pb.

*Outstretched Wings of the Spirit: On Being Intelligently and
Devotedly Religious*
Donald Szantho Harrington
Lenten manual inspired by the rational, naturalistic theol-
ogy of Henry Nelson Wieman and Regina Westcott Wieman.
(UUA) 1980. 116 pp.

The Practical Meditator
Harry C. Meserve
Concise and practical approach to the philosophy and prac-
tice of meditation. (Human Sciences Press) 1981. 137 pp.
Cloth.

Quest
Kathy Fuson Hurt
Personal thoughts on our journey toward personhood,
exploring the quality of human yearnings. 1986 UUA
meditation manual. 71 pp. Illustrated. Pb.

Return to the Springs
Jacob Trapp
A nourishing treat for religious liberals. Explores three
wonderful journeys—prayer, mysticism and holiness—gently
fashioning a new model for spiritual refreshment. (Skinner
House) 1987. 92 pp. Pb.

Speak to the Earth
Ralph N. Helverson
Devotional manual based on the conviction that spiritual
reality is mediated to us in nature as well as in history.
(Ralph N. Helverson) 1955. 63 pp. Pb.

Tao Te Ching: The Wisdom of Lao Tzu
Jacob Trapp
The author shares his interpretations of a first-century
philosopher's wisdom regarding peace, capital punishment,
mysticism and much more. Printed in calligraphy. (Trapp)
139 pp. Pb.

"This Day . . ." Worship Resources for the Liberal Church
Bruce Southworth
Sixty-one readings for worship. Usefully divided: Opening
Words, Chalice Lighting, Prayers and Meditations, Seasonal
and Benedictions. (Rising Press) 1987. 66 pp. Pb.

Three Sermons
Dana McLean Greeley
Traces the Christian, humanist, and Universalist elements
of UUism. Delivered in 1980-1981. (First Parish in Concord, Massachusetts) 16 pp. Pb.

To Meet the Asking Years
Edited by Gordon B. McKeeman
Heartwarming collection of Universalist poetry and prose,
designed to stimulate and guide your personal meditations.
1984 UUA meditation manual. 73 pp. Illustrated. Pb.

A Year with Our Liberal Heritage
Willard C. Frank, Jr.
A real favorite. Fifty-two occasions from the history of
Unitarian Universalism. Perfect for reading aloud. (Unitar-
ian Universalist Advance) 1984. 52 pp. Pb.

About the Author

Jane Ranney Rzepka grew up in Ohio, and graduated from the University of Michigan and Starr King School for the Ministry. After earning a Ph.D. at the Graduate Theological Union and the University of California, Berkeley, she served for four years as Associate Minister in Winchester, Massachusetts. She currently serves the Unitarian Universalist Church in Reading, Massachusetts. She is married to Chuck Rzepka, and they are the parents of two boys, Adam and Toby.